Art Nouveau

Rossana Bossaglia

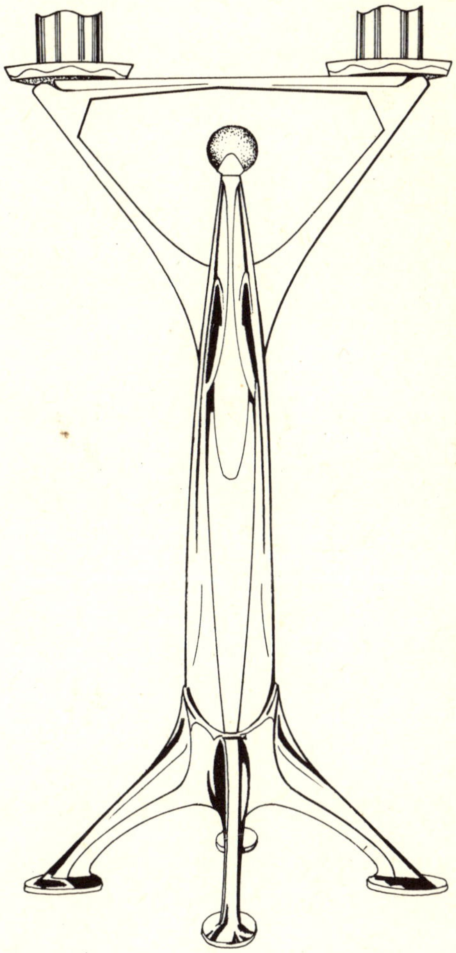

Galley Press

Contents

Published in this edition 1981 by
Galley Press, an imprint of W H Smith and Son Limited
Registered No. 237811 England
Trading as WHS Distributors,
St John's House, East Street,
Leicester, LE1 6NE

Printed in Italy by New Interlitho, Milan
ISBN 0-86136-004-4

The photographs accompanying the introductory section are by courtesy of: Martin Battersby (4, 5, 10); Ferrer's Gallery, London (11); The US Library of Congress (12); Sotheby's Belgravia (7, 8, 13)

Translated from the Italian of Rossana Bossaglia

A new philosophy

The description Art Nouveau is applied to that distinct development in taste which manifested itself at the end of the nineteenth century; partly as a reaction against academic eclecticism (and therefore against the use of decorative formulae which were over-indulged and imitative), and partly as an antidote to the process of industrialization and the apparent loss of aesthetic integrity in mechanically reproduced objects.

Art Nouveau was not, however, a single style derived from a well-defined, clearly delineated area of culture. It was rather a whole series of aesthetic intentions and moralistic preoccupations, manifested in formal attitudes which varied from studio to studio, from hour to hour, and from country to country. Yet despite the contradictory variations in style which can be distinguished, the Art Nouveau movement does present a fundamental unity of dogma resulting from a single original programme.

The new style was not restricted simply to the development of new decorative forms, but was extremely wide in scope – so much so, in fact, that the expression Art Nouveau is obviously inadequate to describe the importance, variety and significance of the products to which it is applied. While taking an interest in these products, the orthodox-minded public refused to take them seriously, and the new style suffered a similar fate in all the countries in which it appeared. The name Art Nouveau was that most widely used for the new style at the time. It was derived from the name of Siegfried Bing's shop which opened in Paris in December 1895 on the corner of the Rue Chauchat and the Rue de Provence. For a number of years before, Bing, in company with a number of other dealers in Paris, had been selling Japanese works of art and now he in particular championed the cause of the new artistic style. In England the name Arts and Crafts was applied to the more conservative English manifestations of the current style, while the name Jugendstil (derived from the magazine *Jugend*) was and still is applied indiscriminately to German and Austrian artefacts.

What then were the principles which made up the common ground of these different manifestations of Art Nouveau? For the first time in history what had hitherto been considered the minor arts became the central interest of the theoreticians and the practitioners; and the discussion of furniture and decoration became principal themes, not merely marginal commentaries in treatises on what are traditionally known as the major arts.

All who advanced theories on Art Nouveau were agreed that artistic activity must be directed to the conception and production of objects for everyday use. Moreover, the new style, divorced of any associations with the past, could be applied to everything from an inkwell to an entire building. This last was one of the main tenets of Art Nouveau, but it is interesting to note with hindsight that the historic styles can still be detected, for instance in French furniture the influence of Louis XV can be seen, and in a number of English silver pieces there was a return to Celtic and Tudor motifs.

Another universally accepted principle of Art Nouveau theory was that a complete synthesis of architectural and decorative elements in an interior could not result from addition of various objects and elements at different times. It was possible only with the systematic and organic application of a formal concept coherently expressed.

The new movement was a reaction against the slavish imitation of past styles mass-produced during the greater part of the nineteenth century and against the fashion for an excessive overloading of interiors with unnecessary furniture and ornaments, often of indifferent quality and design. The Art Nouveau movement thus aimed to invent new forms (a truly revolutionary proposal, for certain styles of a classical type had been considered unchangeable), to stimulate the aesthetic sensibilities beyond the bounds of accepted formulae, and to encourage the conception and realization of an organic unity in design. And a recurrent theme in the leaflets and programmes of the numerous exhibitions of decorative art which took place in Europe from the last decade of the nineteenth century up to about 1910 was just such a refusal, on the part of the organizing committees, to accept for exhibition any work which was purely and simply 'in imitation of a style of the past', and the recommendation that all work should be imbued with an individual style – 'expressive, original, and delicate'.

Behind these stylistic programmes were reformist ideas of a moral and social nature, with roots deep in the consciousness of the new reality that had established itself with the coming of the industrial era. The Art Nouveau artist, devoting himself to the design of small useful objects, accepted a humble work programme that clearly distinguished him from an artist of the romantic type. More important, he demanded that a larger sector of society should enjoy the benefits hitherto restricted to the privileged classes – specifically, the pleasure of living in comfortable surroundings suitable for a decorous and civilized life. He also insisted that this quantitative increase would not be to the detriment of quality, believing that comfort is accompanied by an increase in aesthetic appreciation and that products of utility are inseparable from those of beauty. The most advanced sectors of the Art Nouveau movement – partly inspired by the English aesthetic movement – attributed great importance to the educational influence of beauty. And to prevent the fatal restriction of beautiful objects to the privileged few, they believed that the beauty of an object should be derived not from its rarity or the cost of its materials but from its essential artistic merit.

These new enthusiasts and reformers embraced the principles of Symbolism prevalent in Europe at the end of the nineteenth century and imbued them with new moral strength, making spiritual values concrete and workable. The Symbolists inspired the artistic representation of the mysterious message of nature. And the theorists of Art Nouveau conceived a work filled with beauty in every part, believing that such a world could be a guarantee of freedom, liberating humble and unsophisticated men from the fate of an empty and featureless life.

'La Charmeuse d'Oiseaux' by Georges de Feure, a Dutch-born artist with a fluent and highly distinctive personal style

Craft and commerce

At this point we come up against one of those fundamental anomalies that characterized the Art Nouveau movement and which hastened its end, engendering from one theory so many different movements that the followers of Art Nouveau found them totally irreconcilable.

Those who leaned towards the poetic theories of the English Pre-Raphaelites, and in particular William Morris, planned to safeguard the nobility of the craftsman in everyday production. In past civilizations, and in particular in that of the late medieval world, they recognized a true measure of living in the freedom or the originality of the products of the craftsmen's workshops. They maintained that the artist should not disdain to produce models for common consumer objects and it was often pointed out how Morris designed fabrics, pillows and book bindings – as did, to choose just a few names from the English school, Voysey, Crane, and Bell. These consumer objects should then be made by whoever designed them, or at least under his direct control, since the intervention of any intermediary between the conception and realization of an object might change it or lessen its authenticity.

It was inevitable that such an idea should conflict with the urgent necessity for mass-production on a large commercial scale. Even if the craftsman's product, made of inexpensive raw materials, were offered on the market at a low price – in itself a sufficiently rare occurrence – the fact that such a piece was individually produced would be more than enough to break the rhythm of production. And not only that, the artist or designer could be seen as a corrupting influence. When he worked directly on an object that he had conceived, he produced in most cases a model of exquisite and elaborate workmanship, imbued with a formidable beauty. But inevitably his model was then copied by less dedicated workmen, so that the original's intensity of feeling was frequently diluted.

The most forward-looking and realistic movement of Art Nouveau, widespread in France and above all in the Germanic countries, began from the premise that the machine was the great symbol of the modern age and that it was useless and illogical to ignore it. The artist should rather make the machine his most important implement, using it to apply his ideas to everyday objects produced at reasonable prices for the benefit of as many users as possible. A logical development of this attitude would have been the interpretation of 'form' as something essential enough not to be affected by mechanical repetition, nor by any other process of production, a real reversal of the ideals of the Arts and Crafts Movement and the Symbolists.

Themes from Nature

Two stylistic movements, almost completely opposed, have sprung from the sources of Art Nouveau.

The first, and older of these was born in the world of the Pre-Raphaelites, matured by the flourishes of the French neorococo, codified by the French and Belgian masters who exhibited at Bing's establishment in Paris, and taken over

One of Alphonse Mucha's many famous posters of the great actress Sarah Bernhardt, source of his inspiration and fame

by the German Jugendstil. It made movement its principal characteristic, and attained this by modulations of the floral forms enclosed in a fluid, waving and asymmetrical line. All servile imitations of preceding styles were frowned upon, particularly the false naturalism of the academic classic style, though it was permitted to imitate, or rather compete with, Nature. This was done not only by recapturing life in themes drawn from Nature – scarcely opened flowers, immensely complex insects, and so on – but above all by absorbing Nature's principles and creating vital and diverse new organisms that were capricious and extravagant in appearance but nonetheless based on strict logic. Distant and disparate themes are melted together in the crucible of this style: neogothic, a great deal of neorococo, *japonaiserie* and orientalism of various kinds.

The unity between a building and its interior decoration, the first principle of the whole Art Nouveau world, can be thought of in musical terms as the development of a basic theme, enlarged and modulated in a thousand different ways. This theme can be either floral (the rose, the marguerite, and above all the violet, iris and waterlily), or animal (first of all the dragonfly, the butterfly, the snail, and other insects or molluscs of various species). In the work of the strictest and most creative artists the only trace of naturalistic recognizability is at most a flourish, like the curve of a whiplash or a spiral of smoke, but those animistic characteristics that permit a work's immediate identification with Art Nouveau are nonetheless present.

Some of the most authentic and disturbing masterpieces of Art Nouveau belong to this stylistic movement. They include the architecture, furniture and interior decoration of the Belgian Victor Horta, and (in its earlier phases), of his fellow countryman van de Velde; also of the Frenchman Hector Guimard and the Spaniard Antonio Gaudí. The work of the Scotsman Charles Rennie Mackintosh also belongs here – although his line, liquid and gentle as none other, tended to form geometric patterns relieved by wide smooth surfaces, a feature which brings him near to the abstract geometric school.

This style of Art Nouveau was the first to decline, for it was very dependent on the imagination and ingenuity of artists and on the intrinsic qualities of the materials employed. It was this style though, which, at the turn of the century, excited enthusiasm and passion in Brussels, Paris and Barcelona (and also had important echoes in Russia and Latin America). The general public might be scandalized by it, but this style dominated graphic art and the design of decorative household ornaments throughout the decade of 1895 to 1905.

The triumph of functional design

The second stylistic movement within Art Nouveau also held firm to the principle that interiors must be conceived as a whole and that this unity should originate in the development of a fundamental thematic concept free from all suggestion of 'historicism'. The French and Belgian schools, particularly before 1902, devoted their artistic activity to expression in decorative terms, but other Art Nouveau designers, notably members of the German school, believed that eclectic trifles could be avoided only by concentrating on functionalism of the form. This meant, particularly in architecture, liberation from all unnecessary decoration. This second type of Art Nouveau had many divisions. Some of its adherents, such as Adolf Loos and, in the later stages, Peter Behrens, preached a rigorous functionalism which, contradictorily, tended to be interpreted in heavy and monumental rhythms. Van de Velde practised a bare style anticipating rationalism. Others, like Otto Wagner, Joseph Hoffmann, and Joseph Olbrich, allowed a certain degree of decoration, but subordinated it to strict geometrical rules so that their work, inspired by the Scottish example of Mackintosh and Hugh Baillie Scott, denied all connection with Nature.

It was this style of Art Nouveau which produced the most theoreticians, beginning with van de Velde, a true apostle of Art Nouveau, who in 1894 published his *Le Déblaiement d'Art* (the cleansing of art). Organized into highly ambitious schools, followers of this style devoted particular attention to the architectural aspects of Art Nouveau, which in their hands became not so much a stimulus to the remaking of man's everyday surroundings in the name of beauty, but to the rebuilding of all his cities according to new measurements and new criteria: Art Nouveau was no longer a phenomenon of decorative art, but of civics. In the architectural structures of van de Velde, Horta, Guimard and Gaudí can be recognized the employment on a grand scale of motifs developed for a decorative detail. By way of contrast, decorative details echoing the monumental conception of the whole are characteristic of the work of members of the German school of Wagner (particularly Hoffmann), of several designers for the Palais Stoclet in Brussels, of members of what became the so-called 'Darmstadt colony' (led by Olbrich), and of Frenchmen like Auguste Perret and Russians like Sechtel. In the work of the followers of this group the feeling of a secret life which bubbled up in the products of Art Nouveau was lost, for movement was substituted by dynamism.

New trends in Europe

The most fundamental and unique products of Art Nouveau reveal inspiration from the gothic world, thanks to the theorist and architect Viollet-le-Duc (1814–1879), and an interest in the art of the Far East, particularly in that of the Japanese, masters of functionalism and the complete integration of interior design (the Japanese exhibition in London in 1862 had attracted much attention). They also show the influence of numerous different European social and philosophical movements – so that, inscribed on the banners of the Art Nouveau movement, we find, separately and together, the names of Wilde, Tolstoy, Darwin, Richard Wagner and many others.

The first confrontation between art and industry occurred about 1850, and the Union Centrale des Beaux Arts Appliqués à l'Industrie was founded in Paris in 1863. This confrontation continued and developed with the various exhibitions of applied art which succeeded one another at an accelerated pace in the principal centres of Europe. As time went on exhibitions tended to become more and more 'Universal Exhibitions', not so much in the sense of bringing together the products of the whole world as of being a regular symbol of the march of progress and modern civilization.

New techniques and new developments in the economy made it desirable and necessary to obviate the dangers of industrialization and to exploit its positive aspects in the service of man. Optimists dreamed of a spreading of beauty, made possible by the establishment of a wide market and low prices; but industry, for its part, took the opportunity to produce a multitude of products that had previously been unobtainable or restricted to the rich – so creating fictitious needs and dissipating those forces which would have been better applied to a real reorganization of the 'aesthetic' conditions of the less privileged classes. The splendid revival of wrought iron, for example, of leaded glass, of hollow-ware in glass and ceramics, or of bentwood, which in itself is one of the most attractive chapters of Art Nouveau, very quickly lost touch with the everyday requirements of society and became the mark of the new bourgeoisie, eager for power and for a distinctive sign of its richness, intelligence and broadmindedness.

This deviation of Art Nouveau from its fundamental principles, and so from its original *raison d'être*, is well exemplified in its ambiguous relationship with poster art, following the extraordinary development of lithographic printing in the second half of the nineteenth century. Poster art would seem to be an ideal medium because information – in itself cultural – could be made available to all. But there is no-one who cannot see how at the same time it could be a powerful instrument of persuasion, predisposed to be used against rather than for the general good.

The debate on the relationship between the arts and industry, the flourishing schools of art and crafts, the emergence of reviews devoted to the applied arts – all this, throughout Europe and the United States, preceded the first stylistic proclamation of Art Nouveau. But not only later was this study channelled into the search for new forms of expression.

Some of the first designs anticipating the Art Nouveau style appeared in England, and the English forerunners – notably Dresser and Mackmurdo – possessed an acute subtlety and came from a background with great theoretical awareness. On the other hand the French, in a more instinctive vein, were convinced that the decorative arts had reached their peak of sophistication and elegance in the styles of the eighteenth century, and this inbred conviction showed itself in an unconscious reference to the rococo which proved their limit and their danger and can be seen, for example, in the poster art of Jules Chéret. However the first Arts and Crafts journal in England and *Ornements Typographiques*, by Eugène Grasset, a Swiss transplanted to Paris, were almost contemporary (just after 1870).

It was of the greatest importance that the studies and themes of the individual leaders of Art Nouveau came together at this point in full agreement concerning their place in modern European culture. Les Vingts, a group of twenty artists formed in Brussels in 1884, included in its principles of art some which coincided with the basic principles of the Arts and Crafts movement. In fact both found a common heritage in the concept of the universality of art and the identity of substance of all artistic expression, itself a postulate of Symbolism. The Arts and Crafts movement held their first exhibition in England in 1888; in 1889, at the Paris Exhibition, the French floral style took on its typical neorococo characteristics.

From 1890, for at least a decade, there was not a single artistic event which did not represent another stage in the development of Art Nouveau. So much so that it is essential to restrict ourselves to the observation of what is definitely and avowedly Art Nouveau, avoiding the temptation to dwell on the general atmosphere that exists within the conventionally frivolous characteristics of the *belle époque* and the tough opposition of Symbolism.

In about 1890 the new trends in design spread to the Low Countries and Spain (the first Art Nouveau architecture by G. W. Dijsselhof in Holland, and by Jeroni Granell and Luis Domenech in Barcelona); the first wrought iron designs by, for example, the Belgian Paul Hankar; and the very individual work of Sullivan in the United States.

After 1890 many associations of craftsmen-designers or architect-designers were formed in imitation of the Arts and Crafts. The most illustrious of these were the Architectura et Amicitia of Haarlem and L'Association pour l'Art of Brussels. In 1893 Victor Horta built the Hôtel Tassel in Brussels, designing also every detail of decoration. This building can be considered as the first evidence of a new vision in architecture. Its influence was so profound and

Italian chair by Carlo Bugatti, showing a strong Middle-Eastern influence. A metal disc is suspended by cords from the back frame; both disc and seat contain parchment panels

radical that academic syllabuses were turned upside down, and its vision was so coherent that the outcome was the three-dimensional application of a style that in its early stages had more or less kept to the restriction of graphics.

Also in Brussels – which can therefore be considered the first capital of Art Nouveau as a conscious art form on an international scale – was held in 1894 the exhibition of the Libre Esthétique, an association which gathered together the most avant-garde designers of Northern Europe. This exhibition constituted recognition of a stylistic trend that now transcended the detailed problems of decorative art to occupy the whole field of artistic inspiration. Among the supporters of the Libre Esthétique were: painters like James Ensor with his 'expressionist' style, and Pierre Puvis de Chavannes, a major exponent of so-called 'pictorial idealism'; musicians like Claude Debussy, who wrote for the exhibition his *La Demoiselle Elue*, based on a text by Dante Gabriel Rossetti; Aubrey Beardsley, the unique illustrator of Oscar Wilde's 'Salome'; the Frenchman Aristide Maillol, better known as a sculptor, but who appeared here as a tapestry designer; and the English designer Charles R. Ashbee, founder of the Guild and School of Handicraft. However, the moving spirit of the Libre Esthétique was, together with Ensor, Henri van de Velde, who read his 'Art of the Future' at the opening of the exhibition.

From about 1891, when *La Revue Blanche* (important above all else for the excellence and modernity of its graphics) was founded in Paris, numerous periodicals emerged, bearing the new message. They did not pretend to be reviews specializing in the problems of decorative art – such as would soon appear all over Europe without offering anything very new for the stylistic repertoire. But they did become vehicles of the new taste – keeping the public up to date on the latest developments in Art Nouveau (exhibitions, schools, shops, manufacturers, and the artists themselves), sustaining interest with articles on theory, and exemplifying modern publishing taste in the illustration, layout and typographic design of their pages.

The most important of these periodicals, both for the comprehensiveness of its contents and for the breadth of its approach, was *The Studio*, which first appeared in London in 1893. Its profound influence was felt immediately throughout Europe; in Italy, it inspired the foundation of the *Emporium*, which began publication in Bergamo in 1895.

In 1892 'The Claims of Decorative Art' was published in London by Walter Crane, an intelligent theorist as well as an interesting artist, and this book was followed in 1900 by the fundamentally important 'Line and Form'. Magazines on decorative art began to publish models and alphabets in the new style. In 1892 Georges Auriol published in Paris his 'Le Livre des Monogrammes', which clearly demonstrated the influence of Japanese decorative arts upon Art Nouveau. The alphabet book by the German Otto Eckmann, one of the Jugendstil group, had more to offer and quickly became famous. Most beautiful and distinguished of the magazines referred to, both in its presentation and in the quality of the illustrative material, was probably the Parisian *L'Art Décoratif* (1898–1914). Similar contemporary German periodicals were stricter in their approach but less attractive to look at.

The production of drawing-room objects foreshadowing the Art Nouveau style began in France before 1890 (for example the vases of Leveillé and the early work of Emile Gallé). But the event that made Paris the dazzling centre of Art Nouveau, particularly in furnishing and decoration, was the opening of Siegfried Bing's store in 1895. Most of the principal representatives of the international Art Nouveau style showed their work in Bing's establishment. Among them were Louis Tiffany, the American designer and maker of glass and silverware, and the Frenchmen Georges de Feure, Eugène Colonna and Eugène Gaillard, who contributed to the success of the Art Nouveau pavilion at the Paris Exhibition of 1900. In 1898 Julius Meier-Graefe, a theoretician of understanding and a man of taste, opened La Maison Moderne and procured products designed by van de Velde.

An ormolu lamp by Raoul Larche, depicting Loïe Fuller. This dance star of fin-de-siècle Paris was also a favourite subject of Art Nouveau posters, particularly by Jules Chéret

Art Nouveau in Germany

In the five years between the opening of Bing's shop in 1895 and the Paris Exhibition of 1900, the Art Nouveau style matured and developed under the influence of the French, who continued to favour decoration based on themes drawn from nature. Fine examples are Louis Majorelle's suites of furniture, with their various plant motifs, and Emile Gallé's delicate glass vases and furniture decorated with butterflies and plants (among them an extravagant butterfly-bed). Majorelle and Hector Guimard at their best, elevated the animism and metamorphism of Art Nouveau to heights of fantasy which went beyond any imitation of nature, creating new forms with a mysterious life of their own, that were comparable with those of Horta, van de Velde and Gaudí. But above all, this type of ornamentation became the distinguishing mark of the German Art Nouveau, or Jugendstil, as it is called after the Munich review *Jugend*, founded in 1896.

Jugendstil is essentially a graphic style – and indeed the description 'Jugendstil' is ill-applied to three-dimensional products, even though its influence can be recognized in many objects of the time, particularly in drawing-room statuettes. In Jugendstil a threadlike line, tenuous and waving, takes on the look of long stalks, resolves itself into the petals of a flower, turns upon itself in flowing curves and twists, transforms a woman's hair into vines and creepers, unwinds into flourishes like pools of water to the point of complete abstraction, and then suddenly returns to naturalism in the form of voluptuous waterlilies. All reality seems transformed into a sensual but limpid composition of plant forms; yet this artistic vegetation has no resemblance to the irregular and picturesque explosion of life in nature, following instead its own rules in a hedonistic cult of languid beauty. Unlike the whimsical and fascinating products of Guimard, and certain other leaders of the Art Nouveau movement, which suffer badly if they are imitated, the products of the Jugend movement were more or less depersonalized – although we can recognize artists of outstanding talent, like the Germans Hermann Obrist, August Endell and Otto Eckmann.

The imposing monumental gateway to the Paris Exhibition of 1900. This international exhibition brought together many varied works by the finest exponents of the Art Nouveau style in Europe; together with the better-organized Turin Exhibition of 1902, it marked the height of the movement

In the decline of Art Nouveau, Jugendstil was destined to be the first to become unbearable and corrupted by sickly affectation – or to be revived in hybrid forms like Italian florealism. For this reason the fortunes of Jugendstil scarcely survived the beginning of the new century, and new trends revealed themselves at the Turin Exhibition of 1902.

The last great event

The Turin Exhibition was a great success for the Italians: the exhibits of international Art Nouveau were of the highest quality, and they were more clearly displayed than at the overcrowded Paris exhibition of 1900.

Much of the work shown at Turin belonged to the older style of Art Nouveau. Among the French exhibitors were Gallé, with his unsuccessful dresser in a historic style entitled 'The Great Vine', and the jeweller René Lalique. who showed beautiful combs and buckles with animal and plant motifs. The Italians included Gaetano Moretti, designer for the Milanese firm of Ceruti, and orientalists, with their hybrid folk style, like Carlo Bugatti.

The Belgian school, from Philippe Wolfers to Georges Morren, but led by Victor Horta, with his lively and naturalistic furniture in the original Art Nouveau style, were also at Turin. The first intimation of a new, more abstract style came from the work of van de Velde, a former director of the school of applied art at Mannheim.

Inspired by Scots like Mackintosh, McNair and Taylor, the Austro-German designers made their appearance in markets throughout Europe. Their standards were, however, more commercial. For example, there was no insistence on the collaboration of figurative artists in Germanic furnishing. More important, while still concentrating at least initially on the development of craftsmanship rather than mass-production, groups were supported by an efficient industrial organization which made possible the systematic distribution of numerous products. Important examples of this type of organization were the Vereinigten Werkstätte of Munich and Dresden, founded in 1897–98, and by the Wiener Werkstätte, founded in 1903.

New schools of theory also appeared in Germany, devoted to the study of the relationship between architecture and industrial design. In 1899 the Austrian Joseph Olbrich formed his 'artists' colony' after being summoned to Darmstadt by the Grand Duke, and opened in Weimar the school that was later destined, under the name of the Bauhaus, to play a leading role in contemporary design.

A rare poster designed for the popular Paris store La Maison Moderne, by the Italian artist Manuel Orazi (1902). He designed some of the jewelry worn by the model, whose elaborate hair style is derived from that favoured by Cléo de Mérode, a famous Parisian dancer of this gay period

The work of the Germans and Austrians was not initially well received. Their compact monumentalism repelled the uneducated public, who had scarcely begun to appreciate work of the decorative and elegant French school, and design critics found their work a heavy version of Belgian and Scottish abstract ideas. Nevertheless, these Germanic groups indicated an important direction in design. Objects inspired by the Jugendstil were for the most part a vulgar modification of the fragile, spiritual and disquieting motifs of early Art Nouveau: the furniture and ornaments of the new style (notably the work of Peter Behrens), represent a marshalling of forces against subjects drawn from nature, and were the forerunner of the marvellous developments of the last phase of Art Nouveau.

The Austrian section of the movement, or Viennese Secession, was headed by Joseph Hoffman, and founded in 1897. It represented the most vivacious and pretty tendencies, while still holding rigorously to the abstraction of this Art Nouveau movement. Soon northern Europe, Russia (the architects Sechtel and Zhukov), and Finland (Munc) had adopted the style of the Germans and Austrians.

Italian Art Nouveau designers had a tendency, in their finer exhibits, to lean towards a dignified and abstract style and, while not completely out of sympathy with Guimard, they looked above all to the Anglo-Scottish and the Austro-German schools for inspiration. The furniture of Eugenio Quarti was without severity. That designed by Ernesto Basile for the Palermo firm of Ducrot was lighter but colder – his studio-apartment was remarkable for its functionalism. Italian ceramists were also notable, especially Galileo Chini, as were Italian iron craftsmen, particularly Alessandro Mazzucotelli. The architect Raimondo D'Aronco, designer of the principal pavilions at the Turin Exhibition, also made an important contribution, setting off the various styles and most significant developments of international Art Nouveau with a grace that he rarely achieved again.

Alongside these avant garde Italians of the Turin Exhibition, were others who moved beneath the banner of tradition and nationalism, and brought about the hybrid and characterless style typical of the majority of Italian Art Nouveau. As a result the majority of Italians lost contact with the most effective and lively part of Art Nouveau, with the exception of links with the school of Otto Wagner, and the architecture of early Futurism.

The Turin Exhibition can be considered the last event in which international Art Nouveau is identifiable as a single movement with recognizable characteristics. There were

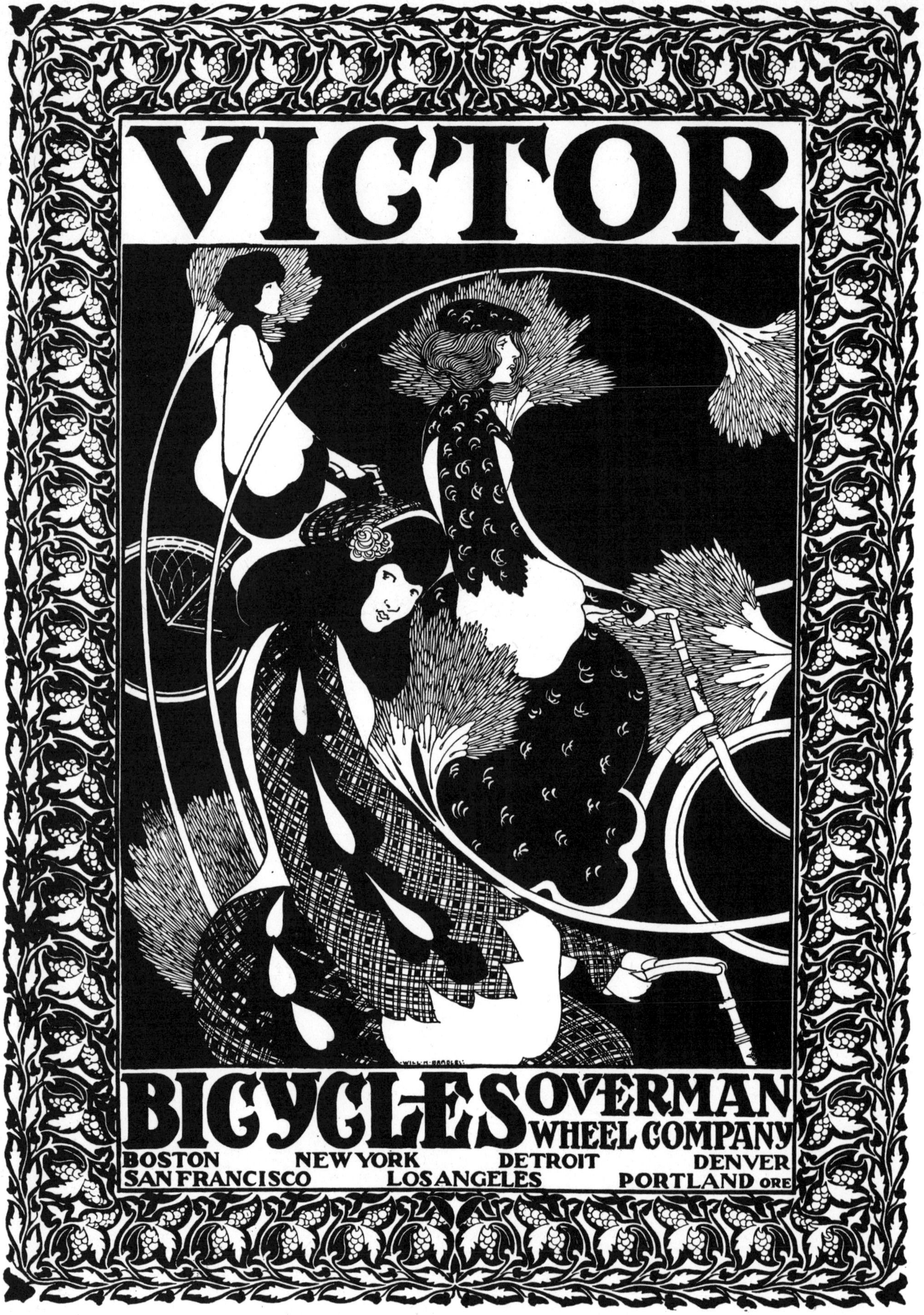
VICTOR
BICYCLES
OVERMAN
WHEEL COMPANY
BOSTON NEW YORK DETROIT DENVER
SAN FRANCISCO LOS ANGELES PORTLAND ORE

Facing page: A delightful lithograph poster for the Overman Wheel Company by Will Bradley (1896). Art Nouveau was not only a European style, but also became popular in America. Above: Silver teapot by Christopher Dresser, one of the English designers whose work anticipated the rise of Art Nouveau. Right: A pair of silver candlesticks by Ashbee, another important English artist who explored the use of Celtic forms. His work greatly influenced the Darmstadt school of Austria

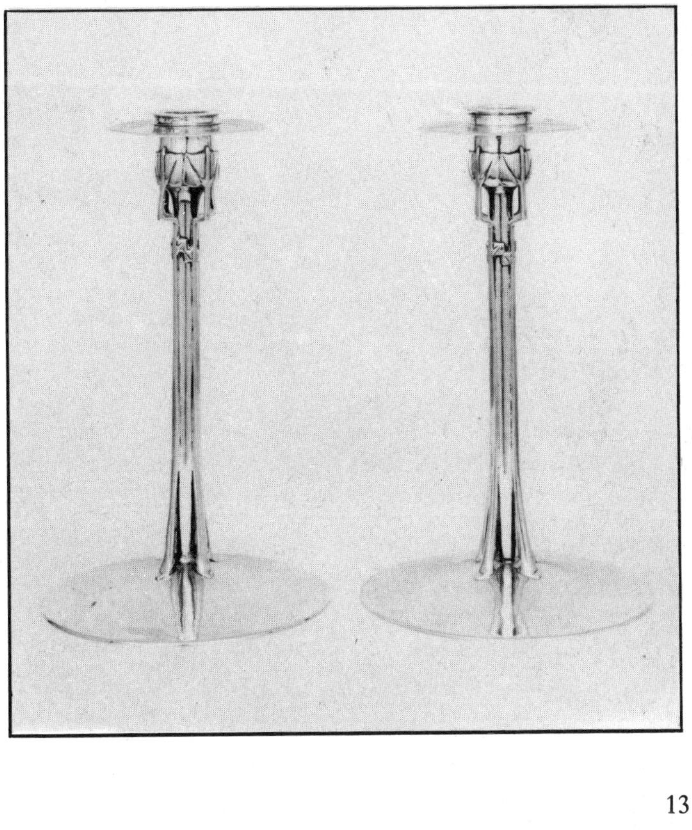

differences between the various schools, but common rules, intentions and manifestos held the movement together. The exhibition was divided into twelve sections, among them a Japanese and an American section, and lacked only a Spanish exhibit to be a complete panorama of contemporary design. The Spaniards had in fact been among the first to receive the message of Art Nouveau. Antonio Gaudí furnished the Casa Calvet in an intensely animistic fashion. The cabinet-maker Gaspar Homar was a close follower of Horta, and Juan Busquets produced work nearer in style to that of Serruier-Bovy and Hankar as well as Guimard and Majorelle. Spanish Art Nouveau long remained related to the earliest style of Art Nouveau – largely because it was dominated by the personality of Gaudí, who offered a unique example with his independent adaptation of the early zoomorphic style of Art Nouveau.

The liberation of art

With only a few exceptions international Art Nouveau in the first years of the twentieth century was directed towards an abstract geometrical and functional style. The less successful attempts at interior design gave way before academic attacks and an impatient reaction against Art Nouveau occurred in various countries. However, the more intelligent and thoughtful modernists pressed forward with discussions on the simplification and gradual formalization of design concepts. They did not deny the path already laid down by Art Nouveau, but wished to see it develop in directions different from those of the last decade of the nineteenth century. The work of the Nancy school provides an important example of this change. Founded as an association of craftsmen by Emile Gallé in 1901, though effectively active for ten years previously, this school was initially particularly inclined toward the floral style of Art Nouveau. From 1902, its work was largely free from naturalistic references. The death of Gallé in 1904 reduced the activity of this excellent school and contributed to the rapid exhaustion of French Art Nouveau – which had already suffered a severe setback with the closing of Bing's Art Nouveau establishment in 1902.

The reign of Art Nouveau was brief and dramatic. The majority of the public hardly had time to marvel at and be scandalized by the audacity of the new style before feeling justified in making fun of it like an out-of-date dress. Its decline was as swift and dramatic as its rise, but this movement which spread throughout Europe and across the Atlantic to North America proved to be the originator directly or indirectly of practically every manifestation of the decorative arts in the first half of the twentieth century. From a distance of half a century we can look back and appreciate its virtues and we can also see its faults, but one thing is clear – Art Nouveau was of the greatest importance in liberating artists and designers from the long bondage of historicism and tradition which had shackled them for nearly a hundred years.

Bibliography

Barilli, R., *Art Nouveau*, London 1969

Battersby, Martin, *Art Nouveau*, Feltham 1969

Blount, B. and H., *French Cameo Glass*, Iowa 1968

Grover, R. L., *Carved and Decorated European Art Glass*, Vermont 1970

Hammacher, A. M., *Le Monde de Henri van de Velde*, Paris 1967

Hiatt, Charles, *Picture Posters*, London 1895

Howarth, Thomas, *Charles Rennie Mackintosh*, London 1952

Hughes, Graham, *Modern Jewellery 1890–1967*, London 1968

Janson, Dora Jane, *From Slave to Siren*, The Duke University Museum of Art, North Carolina 1971

Madsen, S. T., *The Sources of Art Nouveau*, Oslo 1956

Perchan, Emil, *Gustav Klimt*, Vienna 1956

Schmützler, R., *Art Nouveau*, London 1964

The Artist, London 1890–1905 (periodical)

The Studio, London 1893–1905 (periodical)

The Poster, London 1896–1900 (periodical)

Many exhibition catalogues are also of interest. Among the most important are:

Les Industries Artistiques Françaises et Etrangères à l'Exposition Universelle de 1900, Librairie Centrale des Beaux-Arts, Paris 1900

Odilon Redon, Gustave Moreau, Rodolphe Bresdin, The Museum of Modern Art, New York 1962

Der Kunst, Hans, *Secession*, Munich 1964

Stavenow-Hidemark, Elizabet, *Svensk Jugend*, Stockholm 1964

Kunsthandwerk um 1900, Katalog des Hessischen Landsmuseums, Darmstadt 1965

Reade, Brian, *Aubrey Beardsley*, Victoria and Albert Museum, London 1966

Scheffler, Wolfgang, *Werke um 1900*, Kunstgewerbemuseum, Berlin 1966

Die Wiener Werkstätte, Österreichisches Museum für Angewandte Kunst, Vienna 1967

Internationales Jugendstilglas, Museum Stück-Villa, Munich 1969

Jugendstil 20er Jahre, Künstlerhaus-Galerie, Verkaufs-Aufstellung, Vienna 1969

Graham, F. Lanier, *Hector Guimard*, The Museum of Modern Art, New York 1970

L'Art et la Vie en France à la Belle Epoque, Fondation Paul Ricard, Paris 1971

Vienna Secession, The Royal Academy of Arts, London 1971

Index of artists

Although Art Nouveau presented itself in many forms, and comprised a whole series of individual styles, all the best works of the period can be seen to have been inspired by the single unifying concept of revolution in design. In the pages that follow, the unnumbered line drawings – vignettes and decorative motifs culled from contemporary periodicals – have been included to help convey the spirit of Art Nouveau, particularly the new ideas that were formulated in graphics and typography

2 3

1 Pietro Fenoglio. Detail of bow window. Casa Fenoglio, corner of Via Principi D'Acaja and Corso Francia, Turin.

The bow window has been modelled with a delicacy and finesse worthy of a cabinet-maker. This is one of the most beautiful and original buildings of the Italian Art Nouveau style, and was no doubt inspired by the example of Horta; it was completed – as the inscription between the two windows records – in 1903.

2 Pietro Fenoglio. Doorway. Corso Galileo Ferraris 18, Turin.

3 Pietro Fenoglio. Glass door. Casa Fenoglio, Turin.

The motifs of the gracefully asymmetric curved lines reflect one another on either side of the wooden panels and the glass door.

4 Louis Majorelle (1859–1929). End of a balustrade in bronze and wrought iron. Musée des Arts Décoratifs, Paris.

The first phase of Art Nouveau began in France and Belgium; it was characterized by the remarkable fluidity of its motifs, such as the famous ribbon, whiplash and plume of smoke, which were used either in an abstract form or were combined with lively and original stylized plant forms.

Majorelle, a member of the famous Nancy school, produced a series of elegant variations on naturalistic themes. It was from the Nancy school that a succession of pieces of furniture based solely upon floral motifs and of an almost breathtaking virtuosity were produced.

5 Pietro Fenoglio. Staircase landing of the Casa Fenoglio, Turin.

This balustrade is more restrained and less sensual than Majorelle's creation, and was perhaps inspired by the abstract theories of the Belgian Victor Horta. In spite of its greater sobriety, the interior of the Casa Fenoglio clearly shows a unity of style with the exterior façade (see 1). Unfortunately the disfavour into which the style fell has meant that only a few completely Art Nouveau houses have been preserved.

4

5

7

8

6 Firm of Botticelli. Decoration of the Santa Teresa pharmacy, corner of the Piazzale Baracca and the Corso Magenta, Milan.

This is a very valuable example of a building preserved almost in its entirety: an old Milanese pharmacy inside a beautiful Art Nouveau building of 1905. It was the work of the architect Antonio Tagliaferri. The fittings, with their glass panels, are reminiscent of the dry and linear style of the Scottish school and are almost contemporary with the building itself.

7 Gerrit W. Dijsselhof (1866–1924). Room setting. Gemeentemuseum, The Hague.

This is another well-preserved interior. Executed between 1890 and 1895, it shows the characteristic approach of Dutch Art Nouveau, in which medieval motifs were interpreted with great sobriety and resolution. Dijsselhof designed the entire desk, including the beautiful lamp and the tapestries with their representations of flamingos (see 56) and a peacock – creatures also much used in the symbolism of English Art Nouveau.

8 Window. Musée de l'Ecole de Nancy, Nancy.

Quite another spirit animated the artists who established the Art Nouveau school at Nancy. It was one of the best and most exuberant of its time, and is distinguished by its remarkable naturalism, its luxuriance and its choice of motifs which could be called 'neobaroque'. All these elements can clearly be traced in the detail of the window.

9 Victor Horta (1861–1947). Entrance hall. Hotel van Eetvelde, 4 Avenue Palmerston, Brussels.

Glass, like ironwork, played a very important part in Art Nouveau and the combination of these two materials – a sign of the new technological age – was particularly popular with Art Nouveau designers who wanted to show how all materials could be brought to the service of aestheticism. The Hotel van Eetvelde is one of the first works of the famous Belgian architect Horta, and was completed in 1895. Lightness and airiness pervade the whole of this entrance hall
6 on two different levels, divided by a wrought iron balustrade and iron columns.

9

10

12

13

10 Eugène Vallin (1856–1922). Dresser. Musée de l'Ecole de Nancy, Nancy.
This piece forms part of a magnificent and well preserved setting, and can be dated *c.*1905.

11 Eugène Gaillard (1862–1933). Sideboard. Danske Kunstindustrimuseum, Copenhagen.
The style of Gaillard is very different, although it maintains some of the characteristics common to all masters of the French Art Nouveau movement. These are great mobility of drawing, curvilinear statement of theme, tenuous lines linked without interruption, and the resulting incurving corners. While Vallin gave his furniture an architectural plasticity, Gaillard conceived his pieces as a succession of surfaces linked by two-dimensional graphic motifs (in this piece, the typical whiplash motif). This sideboard formed part of Bing's exhibit in the 1900 Paris Exhibition.

12 Louis Majorelle. Cabinet inlaid with various woods. Bethnal Green Museum, London.
This cabinet, with its decoration based on plant forms, is one of Majorelle's most fantastic pieces: an aquatic plant grows from the base towards the top, expands its fronds across the front and frames a small lakeside scene. Art Nouveau furniture produced by first-class craftsmen is distinguished by the subtlety, gracefulness and variety of its details: in this particular example, the locks are decorated with dragonflies. Like the preceding piece it was exhibited in the 1900 Paris Exhibition, was bought by Sir George Donaldson with a number of other pieces and given to the South Kensington Museum, London, for exhibition to craftsmen and students as an example of the finest contemporary design. It was received by a storm of abuse and denounced as immoral and corrupting. Together with all the other pieces it was withdrawn from exhibition and remained hidden in a basement for some fifty years before being finally recognized as the masterpiece that it is.

13 Jean Busquets. Glass panelled cabinet with carved and pokerwork decoration. Museo de Arte Moderno, Barcelona.
The Spanish Art Nouveau cabinet-makers took their inspiration in the first place from their French colleagues. This piece is dated 1907 and the influence of Georges de Feure (see 24) is noticeable.

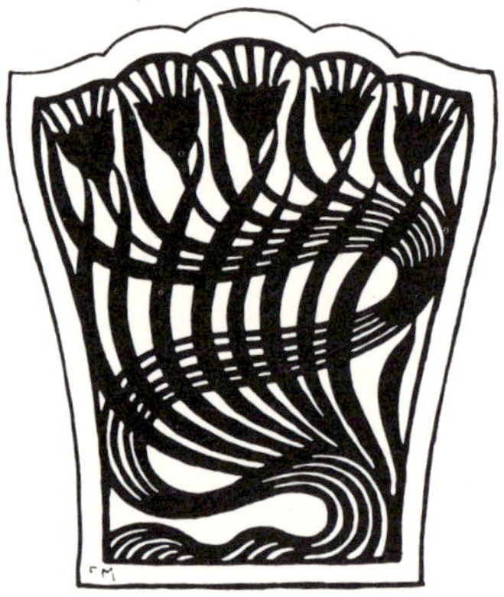

14 Eugenio Quarti. Cabinet with mirror. Malacrida Collection, Milan.

This cabinet is in Eugenio Quarti's style of 1900 to 1903. He was a Milanese cabinet-maker of exceptional talent, and was among the few successful Italian Art Nouveau artists at the Paris Exhibition of 1900. This piece, like others by Quarti at this time, is in mahogany with inlays of mother-of-pearl, silver and gilt bronze.

The small pieces placed on the Quarti cabinet are particularly graceful. The statuette is a gilt bronze version of the famous 'Cothurne' designed by Agathon Léonard for the Sèvres factory. The *cache-pot* was made at the beginning of the twentieth century by the firm of Richard.

15 Ernesto Basile. Secretaire. Galleria d'Arte Moderna, Rome.

This imposing secretaire designed by Basile is an example of the monumental style of cabinet-making more widespread in Italy than the more compact style of Quarti. Basile, an architect, confined himself to conceiving models which were almost always made or at least completed by the firm of Ducrot, in Palermo. This piece is decorated with figurines and ornamental motifs in bronze modelled by the sculptor Antonio Ugo, and the insides of the doors were painted by Ettore Maria Bergler. Virtually contemporary with Quarti's cabinet (see 14), this secretaire was exhibited at the Venice Biennale in 1903.

14 15

16 Gerrit W. Dijsselhof. Dresser (detail of 7). Gemeentemuseum, The Hague.

Dijsselhof's work, dating from the last four or five years of the nineteenth century, follows the dual criteria of simplicity and functionalism. Stylistically, however, this piece shows the influence of medievalism and a certain rusticity which detract from the Art Nouveau quality of its design.

17 Charles Rennie Mackintosh (1868–1928), and Margaret MacDonald (1865–1933). Room setting. (From V. Pica: *L'Arte Decorativa all'Esposizione di Torino del 1902*, Bergamo 1903).

The term Art Nouveau embraces many apparently dissimilar works, for it covers all those linked by historical affinity and by the common ideal on the part of individual designers to produce new forms and to resolve the problems of integrating beauty with everyday life.

Mackintosh is distinguished above all other architects and designers working in Europe at this time for his fluidity and abstemiousness of form. His work reveals a generic affinity with the clarity and treatment of space characteristic of Japanese architecture, and the echoes of ancient Celtic motifs do not detract from the limpid originality of his precise and functional style. The excellence of his workmanship in his best pieces and the delicacy with which carpets, panelling and ironwork were selected in matching colours such as rose pink or green, necessitated constant supervision by the designer-craftsman. Indeed his room-settings have an air of great refinement.

Mackintosh, together with his wife Margaret MacDonald and a number of friends, founded, directed and also designed the buildings of the Glasgow Art School. His work met with considerable opposition in England, where the spirit of William Morris still reigned, but he had a considerable following in Germany and was a decisive influence on the Austrian School. The room design illustrated here was shown at the Turin Exhibition of decorative art in 1902, where Mackintosh's work aroused a great deal of interest.

16

17

18

19

20 21

18 Louis Majorelle. Cabinet, carved with metal appliqué (detail). Bethnal Green Museum, London.

This piece, like the one illustrated in plate 12, was relegated for some fifty years to a cellar in the South Kensington Museum.

19 Emile Gallé (1846–1904). Work table (detail). Victoria and Albert Museum, London.

Rococo was a considerable influence on French Art Nouveau, not because this historic style was directly imitated, but because of a spontaneous sympathy for its asymmetric grace and whimsical curves. The result was a type of neorococo which varied according to the individual skills and personalities of the different artists working in this style.

The work table shown here bears the inscription 'Travail est joie' (work is pleasure). Gallé, like other artists of the period, loved to add such symbolic titles to his pieces.

20 Emile Gallé. Sloping-fronted desk (detail). Danske Kunstindustrimuseum, Copenhagen.

The representational skill of Gallé (who had some renown as a serious student of botany), and his liking for floral compositions in wood and in glass did not diminish his understanding of structural problems. This is clearly evident in the sinuous detail of the leg of this piece, which ends in the form of an abstract leaf. Similar details are also found in the work of Gallé's fellow-countryman, the architect Hector Guimard.

21 E. Baguès (working 1881–1895). Writing table (detail of 35). Victoria and Albert Museum, London.

The extremely naturalistic panels carved with flowers and the dominating curve of this piece have some affinity with the graphic work of Alphonse Mucha.

23

22 Alexandre Charpentier (1856–1909). Cupboard for musical instruments (detail). Musée des Arts Décoratifs, Paris.

Primarily a sculptor specializing in subtle bas-reliefs, Charpentier occasionally designed furniture incorporating gilt bronze plaques, which referred in their subject matter to the purpose for which the furniture was made – in this case to contain a collection of musical instruments. The pale blond wood used here was much in favour with French furniture designers of this period.

23 Gaspar Homar. Central panel of a piece of furniture. Museo de Arte Moderno, Barcelona.

Homar was one of the most brilliant Spanish Art Nouveau cabinet-makers, and worked on more than one occasion with the architect Domenech y Montaner who was in his field second only to Gaudí. The detail illustrated here is from a suite of furniture made for a house by Domenech, the luxurious mansion of Lleó-Morera on the Passo di Gracia in Barcelona.

24 Georges de Feure (1869–1928). Screen (detail). Musée des Arts Décoratifs, Paris.

De Feure was one of the group of outstanding artists who worked for Bing's Art Nouveau establishment in Paris. He was an excellent craftsman with a sensitive and light hand, to whom we owe some of the most delicate pieces of Art Nouveau. His style could be termed neo-Louis XV, and is full of spirit and grace. He was a distinguished draughtsman, and had his own ideas on floral adornment. The screen shown here is typical of his work and was shown at the Paris Exhibition of 1900. It is made of gilded wood and painted and embroidered silk, and shows the delicacy of his composition as well as the dynamic quality of the 'whiplash' revealed in the motif of the curving flower stem.

24

25

26 27

25 Eugène Gaillard. Handles (detail of 11). Danske Kunstindustrimuseum, Copenhagen.
26 Eugène Gaillard. Drawer handle (detail of 11). Danske Kunstindustrimuseum, Copenhagen.
27 Eugène Vallin. Handle (detail of 10). Musée de l'Ecole de Nancy, Nancy.
28 Victor Horta. Lock handle. Hotel van Eetvelde, Brussels.
29 Eugène Vallin. Drawers (detail of 10). Musée de l'Ecole de Nancy, Nancy.
30 Henri van de Velde (1863–1957). Door handle. Nordenfjeldske Kunstindustrimuseum, Trondheim.

The relationship between handles and the furniture to which they are added is of considerable interest. Art Nouveau designers had considerable success in designing furniture fittings as part of the whole. The drawer handles by Vallin emerge like wrinkled cloth from the base plane with astonishing ease (29). Metallic elements can also be unobtrusively incorporated into a piece, repeating the sinuosity, folds, roughness and flexibility of the wooden parts (27). Handles, balustrade handrails (see 4), and similar parts were designed with the anatomical structure of the human hand in mind. The beautiful lock handle by Horta (28) has the appearance of a piece of exquisite ornamentation, but on closer examination it can be seen to meet the precise functional demand of the grip of the hand and the necessity for the lock to move rapidly and smoothly.

29

30

28

31

32

31 Hector Guimard (1867–1913). Three-legged occasional table. Musée des Arts Décoratifs, Paris.

Guimard was the principal architect of Art Nouveau in France. Regarded as a follower and colleague of Horta, he understood and sympathized with Horta's language but interpreted it in his own way. His style is more sensuous than Horta's more abstract style. If Horta uses a zoomorphic motif it is generally a butterfly, dragonfly or some other winged form. Guimard, on the other hand, modelled more fleshy forms – as witness the famous cast-iron and glass station entrances of the Paris Métro.

This attractive occasional table in pearwood, which is part of the furnishing of a bedroom designed by Guimard for the Hôtel Nozal in 1904, has the appearance of a living form in every detail down to the delicate triangular feet. It is easy to understand how such a personal style could prove so disquieting as to provoke the aversion to Art Nouveau that was rife as early as the first decade of the twentieth century, particularly after the First World War. Guimard's style compels one to take sides: one must either love or hate it – and this is no doubt why so much of his work has been destroyed.

33

34

32 Eugène Vallin. Occasional dining-room table. Musée de l'Ecole de Nancy, Nancy.

Compared with Guimard, the attractive work of Vallin appears less creative and vital. Yet Vallin has an unmistakable style, based on openwork curvilinear supports, shapes like the fall of drapery, and details derived from the shapes of ribbons (10, 27 and 29).

33 Eugène Vallin. Office furniture. Musée de l'Ecole de Nancy, Nancy.

The homogeneity of Vallin's style is evident when one compares pieces intended for different rooms: for the dining room (10 and 32) and for the office. This setting was made in Nancy in the early years of the twentieth century for the industrialist Kronberg.

34 Louis Majorelle. Three-legged occasional table. Musée des Arts Décoratifs. Paris.

This three-legged occasional table by Majorelle is in tamarind wood, with floral ornaments in gilt bronze. It is more monumental, powerful and showy than the table designed by Guimard (shown in plate 31).

35

36

35 E. Baguès. Writing table.

This writing table by Baguès shows an eclectic combination of styles: rounded and ephemeral rococo rhythms have been added to a kind of neorenaissance base, with no stylistic equilibrium between the different elements.

36 Gaspar Homar. Side-table. Museo de Arte Moderno, Barcelona.

Strongly reminiscent of the furniture of Gallé and others of the Nancy school, this drawing-room table nevertheless retains a suggestion of Moorish inspiration typical of Spanish work even today. Like 23, it was made for the Lleó-Morera mansion, and therefore dates from 1904 or very slightly later.

37 Three-legged stand in painted and carved wood. Museo de Arte Moderno, Barcelona.

This elegant piece, carved and inlaid with flowers, is stylistically typical of the work of Homar, but cannot be directly attributed to him.

38 Henri van de Velde. Desk. Nordenfjeldske Kunstindustrimuseum, Trondheim.

With the Belgian van de Velde we encounter the works of a master. A painter, graphic artist, author of theoretical writings, as well as an architect and the founder of a school of art and craft, van de Velde influenced the direction of applied art for a whole decade. His earliest works reveal a mobile and vibrant touch and display the butterfly motifs so dear to Art Nouveau. In them van de Velde can be seen to be searching for simplification, a search that showed him to be closer to the experiments of the Scottish school or Englishmen like Voysey rather than those of the Franco-Belgian school.

37

38

39 40

39 Victor Horta. Chair. Hôtel van Eetvelde, Brussels (see 9).
40 Antonio Gaudí (1852–1926). Chair for the Casa Bátlló. Museo Gaudí, Barcelona.
41 Antonio Gaudí. Armchair for a desk in the Casa Calvet. Museo Gaudí, Barcelona.

As an everyday object that must above all fulfil precise functional criteria, the chair provides an excellent demonstration of the experimentation and thinking of the Art Nouveau movement.

Dedicated to the restoration of art in everyday life, the greatest designers of the Art Nouveau movement devoted particular attention to the study of chairs. They had an example before them: the Austrian firm of Thonet which, as early as the middle of the nineteenth century, was manufacturing chairs that were light and harmonious, roomy and eminently practical. There was, however, a psychological difficulty to be overcome: a certain aesthetic attitude which tended to link beauty with 'quaintness'.

Chairs by Horta lacked absolute clarity of design, being elaborate and complex, with excessively modulated lines. Apparently he was determined that no single part should be without movement. The structure of his chairs, however, is light and lively.

Gaudí, the principal exponent of the Catalan school, also showed his brilliant expressionist temperament as a designer of furniture. His chairs seem not so much a response to the requirements of the human frame (suggested by the rounding of the edges, the curving of the chair's seat like a bowl, or the shape of the arms) as to sculptural inspiration. It appears as if all the shapes were moulded with the artist's own hand. Gaudí's furniture might be extremely practical, but it was inspired by a passionate religious and social vision that dominated his whole life.

42 Henri van de Velde and Johan Thorn Prikker. Small armchair. Nordenfjelkdske Kunstindustrimuseum, Trondheim.

The incurving lines of van de Velde's pieces are refined and suggest the idea of comfort – without in fact being comfortable. The spatial movement of the rack-back is reflected in the design of the beautiful fabric made by the Dutchman Johan Thorn Prikker.

Henri van de Velde believed most passionately that art should be unadorned and faithful to the stark beauty of its formal conception and that furniture should be linear yet light. His use of light woods and composite designs came close to the spirit of Mackintosh.

41 42

43

43 Victor Horta. Drawing-room setting. Musée Horta, 25 Rue Amsterdam, Brussels.

Installed in 1899 in the Carpentier villa at Renaix, this setting comprised a suite of furniture in sycamore upholstered in velvet. It is one of Horta's most graceful and successful suites, and typified the unostentatious prosperity of the middle class for whom his work was intended. The motif of the open fantail which inspired the design of the sofa and the armchair and the sliding form of the table legs contribute to the sense of lightness without detracting from the work's sober conception. Such furniture combined well with the cool and narrow palm leaves often employed in Art Nouveau decoration.

This setting is today the centrepiece of what was Horta's home in Brussels. It is now a museum, but is maintained as if it were an inhabited house, with airy rooms wide open to the staircase.

44 Antonio Gaudí. Bench for the Casa Calvet. Museo Gaudí, Barcelona.
45 Georges de Feure. Sofa. Danske Kunstindustrimuseum, Copenhagen.

The bench by Gaudí (44) takes rhythms from the Art Nouveau repertoire – notably the sliding motifs and the moulded appearance of the whole – but the style is completely independent and bordering on 'bad' taste. On the other hand, the sofa by de Feure (45) is delicacy itself and, like his screen (24), is inspired by the style of Louis XV.

44

45

46

47

48

46 Eugène Vallin. Chair. Musée de l'Ecole de Nancy, Nancy.
47 Hector Guimard. Chair. Musée des Arts Décoratifs, Paris.
48 Eugène Gaillard. Chair. Musée des Arts Décoratifs, Paris.

Vallin's chair shows his preference for a baroque approach. The more original Guimard offers here what is superficially an intelligent and lively interpretation of Louis XVI but in which we can recognize his typical motifs – particularly the triangular, almost zoomorphic feet. Gaillard, in this delightful rosewood chair with its original upholstery, presents us with a happy union of lightness, grace and practicality.

49

50

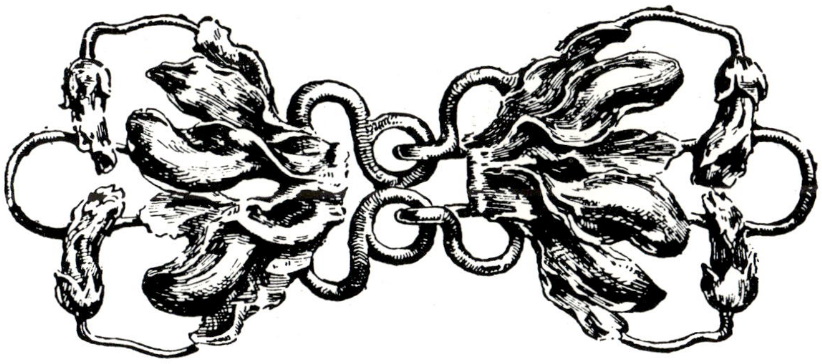

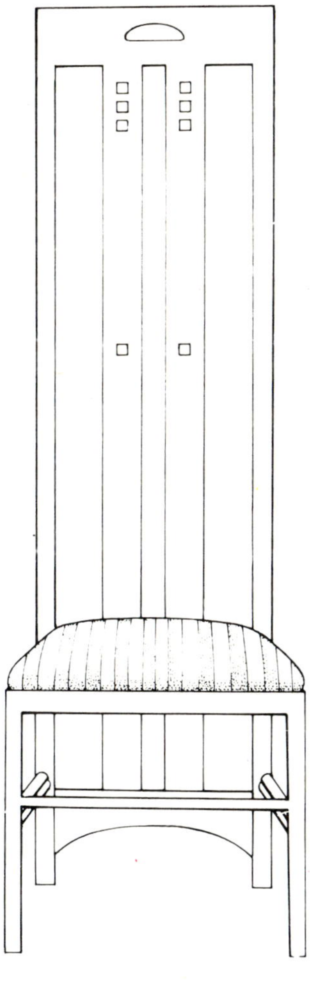

51

49 Johan Thorn Prikker. Chair. Gemeentemuseum, The Hague.
This deservedly famous chair by the Dutch artist Prikker is practical and light and designed according to aesthetic and functional principles. It dates from 1898. Unlike French artists, Prikker did not concern himself with any precious recreation of styles, but sought entirely new forms.

50 Giacomo Cometti. Chair. Property of Paola Cometti, Turin.
Italy was the home of several important workshops owned by craftsmen who were both designers and furniture-makers. The work of Cometti, an Italian cabinet-maker of the first decade of the twentieth century, is particularly interesting. His chairs are remarkable for their grace, practicality and craftsmanship, and they were principally inspired by the work of the Wiener Werkstätte.

51 Drawing of a chair by Charles Mackintosh.
Designers belonging to the Scottish school, and those whom they directly inspired, are characterized by their remarkable sobriety and preoccupation with functional objects. Such a climate, like that in Holland under the influence of van de Velde, encouraged the development of Art Nouveau along rational lines. This design by Mackintosh, with its search for refinement and simplicity, has an almost abstract outline and represents the restoration of geometrical values to interior designs.

52 53

52 Giacomo Cometti. Brass decorations for furniture. Property of Paola Cometti, Turin.
53 Pietro Fenoglio. Door handle in brass (detail of 2). Corso Galileo Ferraris 18, Turin.

Only the finest practitioners of Art Nouveau successfully avoided the very fault that the movement had tried so hard to fight against: a confusion of objects which, although related to one another by a certain degree of common inspiration nonetheless resulted in overcrowded interiors.

These illustrations present a sample of Art Nouveau objects and details chosen from among the most beautiful and most representative of the style. They are not necessarily considered in relation to their contexts.

The function of the delicate brass branches (52) by Cometti is not known but they can be admired as ornaments in their own right.

Fenoglio's door handle (53), with its delicate rhythm in the style of Guimard and its abundant floral decoration, is in perfect harmony with the door (2) and consequently with the whole building (1).

54 Arthur H. Mackmurdo (1851–1942). Screen. Kunstgewerbemuseum, Zurich.

Festoons, draperies and heavy pelmets were eliminated by the Art Nouveau designers, who held them responsible for reducing interior decoration in the nineteenth century to an 'upholsterer's art'. Fabrics were reserved in Art Nouveau for screens or for the upholstering of sofas and armchairs, and fabric wall-hangings frequently gave way to more economical and practical wallpapers.

Illustrated here is a very beautiful screen by Mackmurdo. It is a forerunner of the Art Nouveau movement, with panels woven in silk and gold thread and dating from 1884.

55 Gaspar Homar. Metal hat stand. Museo de Arte Moderno, Barcelona.

Homar's hat stand, shown here against a traditional damask hanging, is part of the famous furnishings of the Lleó-Morera mansion, dating from 1904.

54

55

56

56 Gerrit W. Dijsselhof. Printed linen wall hanging (detail of 7). Gemeentemuseum, The Hague.
57 Owen Jones (1809–1874). Damask. Victoria and Albert Museum, London.
58 Walter Crane (1849–1915). Wallpaper for a child's bedroom. Victoria and Albert Museum, London.

Earlier influences can often be seen in the plant and animal subjects of Art Nouveau designers. The Dutchman Dijsselhof concentrated on the imitation of Javanese batik, and excelled in representations of birds. This tapestry of flamingos (56) belongs to the furnishings of the famous 'Dijsselhof room'. The damask by Owen Jones (57), dating from 1870 or a little after, remains close to classical stylization. And designs by Crane, a great English draughtsman, were closely related to those of the Pre-Raphaelites and so to fifteenth-century gothic.

57

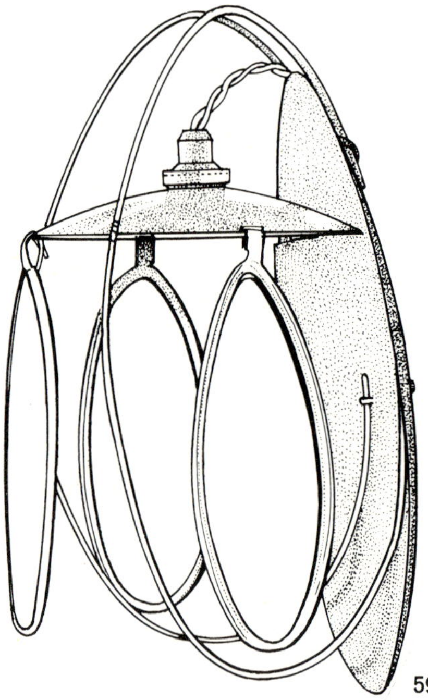

59

60

61

59 Drawing of a wall lamp by Charles Rennie Mackintosh.
60 Gaspar Homar. Chandelier in cast and gilded metal. Museo de Arte Moderno, Barcelona.
61 Eugène Vallin. Bronze and glass chandelier. Musée de l'Ecole de Nancy, Nancy.
62 Alessandro Mazzucotelli. Wrought iron lamp. Private collection, Milan.

The craftsmen and designers of Art Nouveau gratified their wildest fantasies in lamps and chandeliers, combining a worship of technology – as exemplified by the introduction of electric lighting into the home – with a love for fantastic decoration completely divorced from utilitarian requirements.

Some schools encouraged the use of naked electrical apparatus for aesthetic purposes; others, notably the French and Italian, delighted in its transformation into the most curious and fascinating of 'luminous objects'. The Scotsman Mackintosh suggested at the beginning of the twentieth century that lamps should either hang from long electric wires in full view, or be soberly screened with hanging pieces of glass (59). His influence was felt over a wide area, but most decorators attempted an intermediate solution, leaving the wires in view but enlarging and complicating the light shades.

Very different from Mackintosh's work is that of the masters of the French, Spanish and Italian schools. Vallin designed his fine chandelier (61) as part of the baroque-style decoration of his justly famous dining room (see 10); its glass is the outcome of his collaboration with the studio of the Daum brothers at Nancy.

The Spaniard Homar was inspired by tradition to design a lamp suspended from fine metal chains (60). It is decorated with slender dragonflies.

62

63

64

64 M. Bouval (died *c.*1920). Gilt bronze candlesticks. Galleria del Levante, Milan.

Bouval was another French designer who stayed faithful to the favourite themes of the golden age of Art Nouveau (the last five years of the nineteenth century). Featured in his work were young girls combined with flowers, young girls transformed into flowers, or as in this particular example, sensuous caryatids supporting enormous tulips. The flowing lines, the sleek and gentle modelling and the glossy surfaces of these candlesticks have the appearance of melted wax.

65

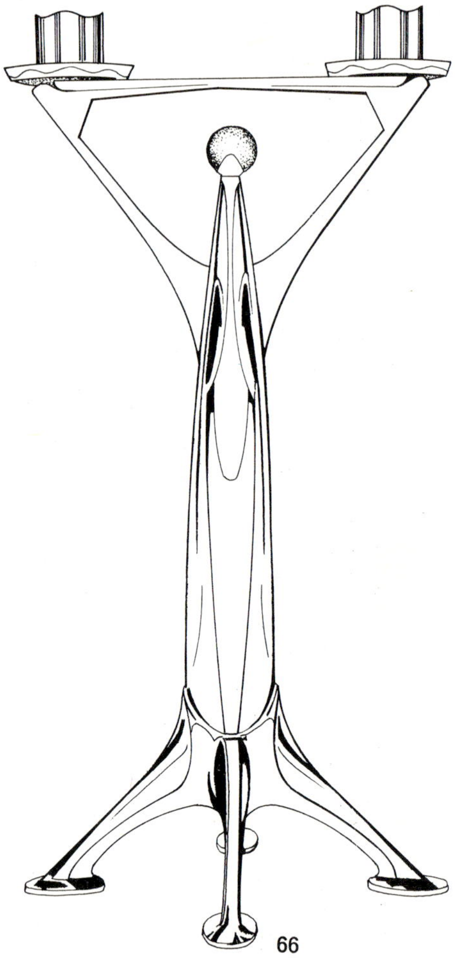

66

67

68

69

70

65 Candelabra of gilded metal. Galleria del Levante, Milan.
66 Drawing of a candelabrum by Joseph Olbrich.

The gilded metal candelabra (65) represent a return to the neo-Celtic taste and to shapes that were less obvious than those of the gothic revival that was gradually going out of fashion. Candelabra of this type provided the inspiration for the fine example designed by Joseph Olbrich (66), a master of the Viennese Secession, in 1901.

67 Alejo Clapés. Drawing room mirror. Museo de Arte Moderno, Barcelona.

Art Nouveau designs for mirrors were numerous, varied, and sometimes over-experimental. This Spanish example, made for the Casa Ibarz, has a lively and streamlined shape but somewhat excessive tangles of carved wooden branches.

68 'Memento' bronze figurine. Collection of Piero Bianconi, Minusio.

Small objects and curios often had symbolic themes in Art Nouveau. Such themes, with explanatory titles and Latin mottoes, were particularly common in the French and Italian schools, but they were also frequently employed in a more stylized form, in the German Jugendstil.

69 Gilded flower vase. Galleria del Levante, Milan.

Italian Art Nouveau is often accused of a certain heaviness, but this flower vase has a refined fluidity. It can be attributed to the last years of the nineteenth century.

70 Studio of Celestino Fumagalli. Ashtray in cast metal. Private collection, Milan.

This ashtray comes from the workshop of Fumagalli, a gifted sculptor and goldsmith working in the Italian Art Nouveau manner in Turin.

71

72

71 Seligman silverware, Manusardi collection, Milan.
72 Silver card holder. Private collection.

Continental Art Nouveau silver can show striking resemblances to naturalistic silver objects from the Louis XV period, and this plate (71), with its asymmetrical design of flowers and bullrushes affords a fine example.

The card holder (72) resembles objects made in France and above all in Germany (for example by Martin Mayer at Mainz). It is, however, possible that it was made in Italy, for its poppies resemble those by Fenoglio (see 2).

73 Metal inkstand. Danske Kunstindustrimuseum, Copenhagen.
74 Henri van de Velde. Brass inkstand. Nordenfjeldske Kunstindustrimuseum, Trondheim.

Art Nouveau designers did not confine themselves to precious metals but also used metals like copper, brass and iron that had hitherto been considered as largely utilitarian or suitable only for sculptors or craftsmen like locksmiths. Now designers like Ashbee and van de Velde showed that it was possible to use these metals for miniature works of art of a kind that would formerly have been made only of precious metals.

75 Charles R. Ashbee (1863–1942). Silver spoon. Kunstgewerbemuseum, Zurich.

This serpentine spoon by Ashbee is both practical and aesthetic.

76 Drawing of a place setting by Joseph Hoffman.

This admirably concise place setting was designed in 1904 by Hoffman, one of the finest designers of the Wiener Werkstätte. It represents the development in Art Nouveau towards simple, functional models that might easily be mass-produced.

73

74

75

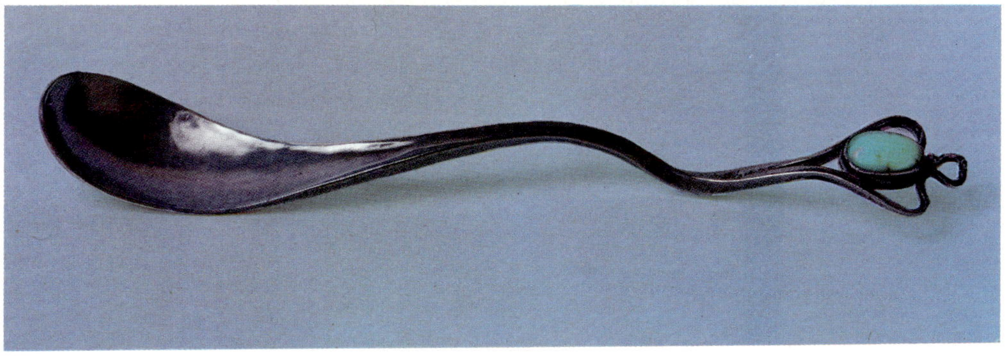

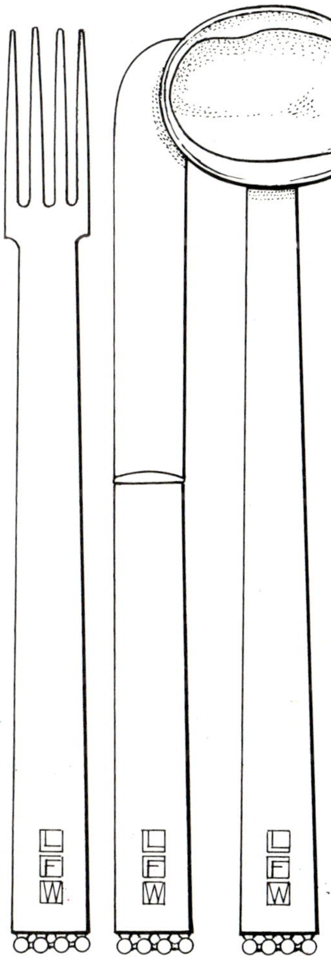

76

77

78

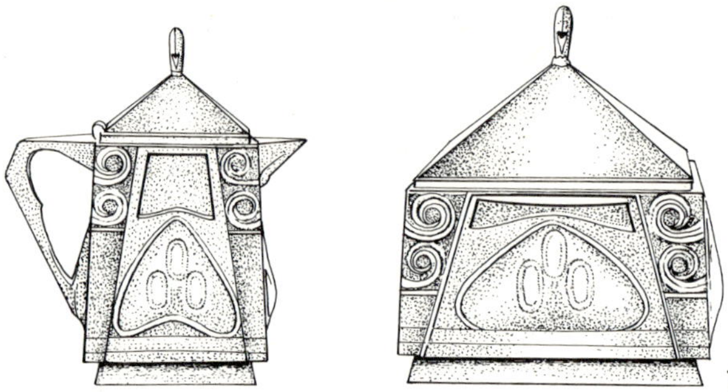

79

80

81 82

77 Charles R. Ashbee. Silver lid. Kunstgewerbemuseum, Zurich.
78 Charles R. Ashbee. Silver mustard pot. Kunstgewerbemuseum, Zurich.
79 Drawings of a teapot and sugar bowl from the Darmstadt school.

Pieces by the Englishman Ashbee, compared with those of the French school or Jugendstil, appear very deliberately simple. They are of considerable value, not only because of the richness of the material but also because of the great care taken by the silversmith and the ingenious way in which the geometrical requirements of symmetry and lighthearted irregularity have been combined. Ashbee, partly inspired by the neo-Celtic formula and the example of the Glasgow school, worked towards a rigorous purification of form in the years 1900–03. With Mackintosh, Ashbee was a major influence on the Austrian Secessionists, particularly on the Darmstadt school founded by the Viennese Olbrich under the patronage of the Grand Duke of Hesse.

80 Emile Gallé. Tray of carved and inlaid walnut. Victoria and Albert Museum, London.
81 Karl Koepping (1848–1914). Glass cup. Danske Kunstindustrimuseum, Copenhagen.
82 Carlo Testa. Card tray of carved wood. Property of Paola Cometti, Turin.
83 Felix Braquemond. Pottery plate. Musée des Arts Décoratifs, Paris.

The subtle shape and delicate inlay of Gallé's wooden tray (80) reveal not only his interest in botany but also his influence by Japanese design. The card tray by Carlo Testa (82) can be dated as late as 1915. It shows an entirely different approach to the use of floral motifs and lacks the grace and elegance of its earlier French counterpart.

The glass cup by the German Koepping (81) has the form of a flower and is executed with exceptional naturalness and lightness. It dates from 1896.

Braquemond's pottery plate (83) dates from 1867. It has been regarded as one of the forerunners of Art Nouveau, with its asymmetrical Japanese-inspired decoration of honeysuckle and a ribbon motif anticipating the 'whiplash' so popular with Art Nouveau designers. It is embossed with typical rococo motifs.

83

84

85

86

84 Emile Gallé. Glass vase with floral motifs in relief. Musée des Arts Décoratifs, Paris.
85 Emile Gallé. Glass vase with transparent and relief chinoiserie decorations. Musée des Arts Décoratifs, Paris.
86 Emile Gallé. Crystal and enamel vase with animal motifs. Musée des Arts Décoratifs, Paris.

Some of the most brilliant Art Nouveau pieces were vases, particularly those made of glass. The greatest master of Art Nouveau glass was undoubtedly Emile Gallé, leader of the Nancy school. His skill in glass techniques kept pace with an imagination that was always in search of new modes of expression. From transparent vases (86), which belong on the whole to his pre-Art Nouveau period, he went on to vases of thick, opaque glass on which he obtained transparent or relief figures with acid or the introduction of cobalt oxide, gold dust or other materials. His floral compositions were unsurpassed – as were the dragonflies and butterflies on the smooth surface of his vases. Gallé also enjoyed experimenting in the various vagaries of contemporary taste, manufacturing 'Chinese' vases (85), or extravagant jugs in the baroque style (91). On his vases, Gallé's signature, in letters inspired by Japanese calligraphy, is often accompanied by a line or quotation from a contemporary poet such as his patron Robert de Montesquiou or from the poetess Anna de Noailles.

87 Studio of Emile Gallé. Two lamps in glass and bronze and a glass shade. Private collection, Milan.

Gallé opened a workshop in Nancy in 1890 to produce his glass on an industrial scale, so making it available in a much wider market and at more reachable prices. Products from this workshop were all of excellent quality and bore Gallé's name.

88

89

90

91

88 Louis C. Tiffany (1848–1933). Blown glass vases. Museum of Modern Art, New York.

Another famous master of Art Nouveau glass was Louis Comfort Tiffany, who maintained close contact with the French school, exhibited at galleries in Paris and worked for the Maison Bing. He was interested in a wide range of craftsmanship, including ceramics, jewellery and wrought iron, but it was in glass, and particularly in blown glass, that his brilliance was fully revealed. Although influenced by the work of Gallé, and perhaps also by that of Koepping, Tiffany's products bore the full imprint of his own personality in their irregularity of form and subtle vibrance. To his own patent glass, with its opalescent and iridescent colouring, reminiscent of Turkish or Persian pottery, he gave the name *favrile*.

Something of the variety of Tiffany's work can be seen from these examples, all made in 1900: a flower-shaped cup with its fine and delicate colouring (centre); an oriental-style vase, with its rich iridescence (left); and a small vase resembling an old ointment pot (right).

After 1900, Tiffany began production on an industrial scale, lending his name directly to a particular style of glass-making. The workmanship of these products is, however, excellent, and they are of considerable value.

89 Vase of iridescent glass, possibly by Loetz. Private collection, Milan.
90 Glass jug, English *c.*1820. Victoria and Albert Museum, London.
91 Emile Gallé. Glass jug with metal mount. Musée des Arts Décoratifs, Paris.

The iridescent stripes in the vase that is possibly by Loetz (89) continue a tradition of a blown-glass technique which had been known as far back as ancient Egypt and which can be seen in a similar version made in England in about 1820 (90).

The sumptuous jug designed by Gallé (91) is quite different. Resembling some of the classic pieces of the sixteenth century, this is a truly exceptional product, particularly since the inventiveness of Gallé is more typically represented in the transparency or opalescence of his better-known pieces (84, 85 and 86). The metalwork was contributed by Joseph Joindry and François Perraux.

92

93

92 Christopher Dresser (1834–1904). Glass jug mounted in silver. Victoria and Albert Museum, London.

Dresser is considered, along with Mackmurdo and other masters of the British school, as one of the forerunners of Art Nouveau. It is easy to recognize in the subtly zoomorphic form of this glass jug's mounting, and particularly in the paw-like feet, the precursor of Ashbee and a whole succession of Art Nouveau designers.

93 F. Venturi. Glass bowl with pewter mounting. Property of Paola Cometti, Turin.

Art Nouveau designers enjoyed combining different materials in one object; presenting surprising contrasts, showing that unity of style could be achieved with different materials, and testing their ability and virtuosity in the development of new techniques.

In this bowl by Venturi, the glass provides a three-dimensional form while the metal's function is purely graphic. In the jug by Dresser (92), the two elements play complementary parts in the structure of the object.

Glass was also used effectively by Art Nouveau designers for stained glass windows. These were almost always in several colours, and were used to divide the street entrance from the inner door in private houses.

94 Paul Gauguin (1848–1903). Ceramic vase. Musées Royaux, Brussels.

Another important Art Nouveau development was the flowering of ceramic art and the development of new and audacious techniques and procedures in this field. In *L'Objet 1900*, Maurice Rheims included the following artists among the finest French ceramists: Décorchement, who designed very thin-walled vases, Dammouse, who worked with hard paste Limoges porcelain, and several

94

masters of the still famous Sèvres factory. Georges de Feure, Eugène Colonna and Auguste Delaherche all made ceramic works for Bing, and other great names were Thesmar and Leveillé. The quantity and quality of the products of these French craftsmen is unquestionable, but all the principal European schools of Art Nouveau also worked experimentally in ceramics and examined new techniques.

It would be a difficult task to list all the craftsmen and designers who made ceramics, for almost all graphic artists, architects, painters and even sculptors belonging to the Art Nouveau movement at some time made objects in ceramics. Auguste Rodin, when a young man, worked for the Sèvres factory. This enchanting vase was made in 1888 by Paul Gaugin, who took advantage of the properties of the material to realize an original version of the pictorial technique of *cloisonné* – distinct areas of colour enclosed by thick lines like the leading of a window.

Traditional manufacturers monopolized the services of famous artists for their designs, and at the same time new factories and new specialists emerged. In Holland, the Rosenburg works made use of the brilliant designs of Théodore Colenbrander, who revived Javanese motifs, as well as the more delicate work of Kok, who was inspired by the flower and animal themes of the Far East.

In Italy, Galileo Chini founded 'L'arte della ceramica' in Florence, and at the same time the combination of Giulio Richard with the old-established Ginori works resulted in the most elegant and captivating Art Nouveau products. From these factories came not only vases but also a succession of ceramic tiles which were widely used for the decoration of interiors and exteriors of buildings, following the example of Otto Wagner in Vienna after 1897. A small but outstanding example of tiling decoration is the interior of the pharmacy in Milan (see 6).

95

95 Group of ceramics. Private collection, Milan.

The collection of objects in the Italian Art Nouveau style is particularly difficult because, with the exception of certain old-established factories which have preserved examples in their own museums (like the firm of Richard-Ginori, who have a famous museum at Doccia), most of these objects have, unfortunately, been dispersed and destroyed.

Among the works that have survived are delicate vases by Galileo Chini who, from the last years of the nineteenth century, raised his ceramic works at Florence to international standing, reviving the ancient craft of *faience* and introducing new ideas from the East, from Jugendstil, and from the Secessionist Klimt.

The vases illustrated here come from different sources and are nearly all anonymous. The one in the centre, decorated with a life-like dragonfly, is Italian, as is the bowl in the foreground. The bowls decorated with marguerites and with maple leaves are signed J. Ekberg and come from the Swedish Gustafsberg factory, which had considerable success at the Turin Exhibition of 1902. They date from 1897–9. The tall narrow vases at the back come from the Amsterdam works of De Distel, and can be dated about 1905; among the many Dutch masters who worked in this style was van der Hoef.

96 Emile Gallé. Vase standing on a dresser by Eugène Vallin (10). Musée de l'Ecole de Nancy, Nancy.
97 Mugello factory (Galileo Chini). Vase in metallic lustre ceramic. Property of Paola Cometti, Turin.

This beautiful piece by Gallé (96) is seen here in surroundings of his choice: the famous dresser by Vallin at Nancy (see 10), which also bears a set of ceramics by the Daum brothers. Gallé and the Daum brothers have totally individual styles, but it is nevertheless evident that they were part of the same movement.

Galileo Chini designed many vases in stoneware produced by various techniques; but his speciality was metallic lustre. His oriental designs, which were glazed with rich and velvety colours, are particularly highly valued. The factories that mass-produced his work understood how to retain the freshness and delicacy of his patterns and above all maintained a high degree of technology in the service of a decorative concept that was never banal or mechanically repetitive.

96 97

98 99

100

98 René Lalique (1860–1945). Brooch in gold, enamel and semi-precious stones. Musée des Arts Décoratifs, Paris.
99 Henri and Paul Vever. Jewelry in gold, enamel and precious stones. Musée des Arts Décoratifs, Paris.
100 René Lalique. Pendant of pearl, gold and enamel. Musée des Arts Décoratifs, Paris.

Although jewelry is not strictly a part of interior decoration, there is nevertheless an affinity between Art Nouveau jewelry and the various contents and decoration of the dwellings contemporary with it – mainly because houses and personal ornaments were made with the individual's personality in mind, and because both reflect the movement's ideal that all detail should be an intrinsic part of the whole.

The designs of the goldsmiths and jewellers of the Art Nouveau movement were exceptional in their originality. One of the great talents of the Art Nouveau period was undoubtedly René Lalique, whose jewelry – with its combination of enamel, precious and semi-precious stones and even carved or moulded glass – glowed with colour and was revolutionary at a time when rich women favoured diamond jewelry almost exclusively. Extremely light in design, his work is superb in its technical finish and it is not surprising that almost the entire exhibit which he contributed to the 1900 Paris Exhibition was bought by Calouste Gulbenkian and is now on exhibition in the Gulbenkian Museum in Portugal. Lalique collaborated with the famous poster designer Mucha in jewelry for Sarah Bernhardt, which first brought his name to the attention of the public early in the twentieth century. He gave up jewelry in favour of glass-making, achieving an equal reputation in this field. The other piece illustrated here (99) is by the Vever brothers who were also imaginative craftsmen of the highest quality.